Money and Politics

FINANCING OUR ELECTIONS DEMOCRATICALLY

David Donnelly, Janice Fine, and Ellen S. Miller

Foreword by GORE VIDAL

Edited by Joshua Cohen and Joel Rogers
for *Boston Review*

BEACON PRESS
BOSTON

BEACON PRESS
25 Beacon Street
Boston, Massachusetts 02108-2892
www.beacon.org

Beacon Press books are published under the auspices of the
Unitarian Universalist Association of Congregations.

© 1999 by Joshua Cohen and Joel Rogers
ALL RIGHTS RESERVED
Printed in the United States of America

05 04 03 02 01 00 99   8 7 6 5 4 3 2 1

This book is printed on recycled acid-free paper that contains at least 20
percent postconsumer waste and meets the uncoated paper ANSI/NISO
specifications for permanence as revised in 1992.

Text design by Christopher Kuntze
Composition by Wilsted & Taylor Publishing Services

Library of Congress Cataloging-in-Publication Data

Donnelly, David.
    Money and politics : financing our elections democratically /
David Donnelly, Janice Fine, and Ellen S. Miller ; edited by Joshua
Cohen and Joel Rogers for the Boston Review.
      p. cm. — (The new democracy forum)
  ISBN 0-8070-4315-X (pbk.)
    1. Campaign funds—United States. I. Fine, Janice. II. Miller,
Ellen S. III. Cohen, Joshua, 1951–   . IV. Rogers, Joel, 1952–   .
V. Title. VI. Series.
JK1991.D67 1999
324.7′8′0973—DC21   98-53710

Contents

Foreword by Gore Vidal / vii

Editors' Preface by Joshua Cohen
and Joel Rogers / xiii

I

DAVID DONNELLY, JANICE FINE,
AND ELLEN S. MILLER
Going Public / 3

II

SENATOR RUSSELL FEINGOLD
Modest Reform? / 33

ZACH POLETT
Empower Citizens / 42

DOUGLAS PHELPS
Setting Limits / 49

E. JOSHUA ROSENKRANZ
Clean and Constitutional / 60

STEVE ROSENTHAL AND AMANDA FUCHS
Labor's Role / 65

BRUCE ACKERMAN
The Patriot Option / 69

THOMAS E. MANN
A Plea for Realism / 74

DANIEL H. LOWENSTEIN
A Role for Parties / 78

III

DAVID DONNELLY, JANICE FINE,
AND ELLEN S. MILLER
Reply / 87

Notes / 92

About the Contributors / 96

Foreword

GORE VIDAL

On a recent cross-country tour of the U.S., I chatted about politics with all sorts of audiences—sometimes in the flesh, more rarely from the tube, where I once reigned but now, as our rulers grow edgy, am relegated to the cable margins (along with such fellow nay-sayers as Noam Chomsky). In these conversations I found again, despite ever greater media censorship of radical ideas, that my audiences were quite alert to the perfect corruption of our public life. They know that political offices are bought by those who can pay and denied to all the rest, that politicians are better identified with their corporate ancestry than voting base (the late Senator Henry Jackson, for example, being more accurately described as the senator from Boeing than Washington state). But, given this, I was often asked: "Why is nothing done?" "Why is there so little outrage?" "Why is there no party of Reform?"

Why indeed? Writing in 1758, David Hume observed, "Nothing appears more surprising to those who consider human affairs with a philosophical eye than the easiness with which the many are governed by the few, and the implicit submission with which men resign their own sentiments and passions to those of the rulers. When we inquire by what means this wonder is effected, we shall find out that, as Force is always on the side of the governed, the governors have nothing to support them but opinion. It is, therefore, on opinion only that government is founded, and the maxim extends to the most despotic and most military governments as well as the most free and popular."

To deny inconvenient opinions a hearing is one way the few have of controlling the many. But as Richard Nixon used to say, "That would be the *easy* way." The slyer way is to bombard the public with misinformation. During more than half a century of corruption by the printed word in the form of "news"—propaganda disguised as fact—I have yet to read a story favorable to another society's social and political arrangements. Swedes have free health care, better schools than ours, child daycare centers for working mothers ... *but* the Swedes are all drunks who commit suicide (even blonde blue-eyed people must pay for such decadent amenities). Lesson? No national health care, no education, etc., because—as William Bennett will tell you as soon as a TV red light switches on—social democracy, much less socialism, is just plain morally evil. Far better to achieve the good things in life honestly, by inheriting money or winning a lottery. The American way.

The fact that the United States was never intended to

Foreword

be a democracy is so well known that it is now completely forgotten. (Hence the familiar, grinding incantation of our opinion makers: "We are the greatest democracy on earth, with the widest range of detergents, etc.") The most candid of the Founding Fathers, John Jay, put their opinion on the matter in an artless but truthful way: "The people who own the country ought to run it." James Madison, a preacher's son, poured unction over this when he acknowledged demurely and approvingly the iron law of oligarchy that invariably comes to govern parliaments, congresses, and nations. The few will always control the many through manufactured opinion, which bedazzles and confuses the many when it is not just plain dumbing them down into the dust of what Spiro Agnew called "the greatest nation in the country."

Nevertheless, a truly *popular* opinion is beginning to coalesce in the perpetual shadow of manufactured opinion: our system of electing politicians to office is rotten and corrupted to its core, because organized money has long since replaced organized people as the author of our politics. And most of it comes from rich people and corporations, who now own our political process—lock, stock, and pork barrel.

Some nuts and bolts. Of the billions now spent each election cycle, most is donated in checks exceeding $1,000. But less than one-tenth of 1 percent of the general population make individual contributions at this rate. And among group contributors, better than 90 percent comes from corporations, which duly record their political investment as a tax-deductible "cost of doing business." These happy few are prepared to pay a high and rising price for the privilege of controlling our government. In the 1998 election cycle, the average winning House candidate cost the owners about $900,000, the average winning Senate candidate a bit over $6 million. Multiply both figures by two if you want the cost of dislodging an incumbent from office—in a system where, last time around, over 97 percent were reelected. To finance a race in big media markets like New York or California, it's a bit more expensive: as of election day 1998, something like $36 million and $21 million respectively.

And if they tire of buying others, of course, the rich can buy political offices for themselves. In its truly Caligulaesque *Buckley v. Valeo* decision, our Supreme Court, ever eager to extend their eccentric notion of democracy, ruled that the rich have every right to spend as much of their own money as they like to buy an office. Hence, a demi-billionaire like Herb Kohl could campaign as "Nobody's Senator but Yours!", meaning not "yours" but "mine," and win.

Do the many really hold the opinions of the few who own the political process? It would seem not, since only half the eligible voters can bring themselves to vote in a presidential election, while only a third vote in off-year congressional elections.

On dark days I incline to what Henry Adams wrote at

Foreword

the start of "our" century: "The whole fabric of society will go to wrack, if we really lay hands of reform on our rotten institutions.... From top to bottom, the whole system is a fraud, all of us know it, laborers and Capitalists alike and all of us are consenting parties to it." Thus, business—Henry Adams's "it"—gets back much more from government than it actually invests in the process while the citizens don't even get a national health service.

The essays collected in this volume set out to illuminate—even undo—the "wrack." Why should we allow our admittedly fragile democracy to be for sale? Without limiting political debate, why don't we put ourselves to the task of sharing its costs so that elections would be more open and freely contested? On a per capita basis, those costs would be trivial—a few dollars a year. And by what hypocrite's indulgence could we not do this, and still call ourselves democratic? Reforms are working in the state of Maine. Why? Discuss. Will they work on a vast scale, in California, say? The US of A? Herewith, some new opinions and facts to challenge the current superstitions about our estate, its owners, and alternative means of management.

To be sure, curing the evils of campaign finance will not solve all of America's other problems, but without such reform it is difficult to see how those other problems can even be addressed, much less dealt with.

This book—full of the experience and hope of activists now struggling to reform our campaign finance system, and the perspective of academic students of it —suggests a number of ways such reform might be achieved. It is the most informed and accessible discussion of the issue that I have seen to date. "Although the heart of man is made to reconcile the most glaring contradictions" (Hume again), now let us use our *heads* and deal appropriately, as they say in Washington, with a corporate ruling class that has hijacked the nation, and in so doing eliminate at least one glaring contradiction: that ours is a government of, by, and for the many when it is so notoriously the exclusive preserve of the few.

Editors' Preface

JOSHUA COHEN AND JOEL ROGERS

Elections are now for sale, and most Americans are not happy about that fact. Whatever their shifting approval of individual politicians, super-majorities of the public are constant in their belief that the system by which those politicians are elected is deeply corrupt. And of course they are right.

Familiarly, the principal source of corruption is the growing and now overwhelming role of money in elections. While money has always been the mother's milk of campaign politics, in recent years it has effectively crowded out other sources of political power. Labor-intensive campaign techniques (door-knocking, precinct organization, etc.) have been largely replaced by capital-intensive ones (TV ads, continuous polling, direct-mail prospecting for support, etc.). The result is a system in which the ability to raise large sums of cash is the threshold and enduring test of a candidate's viability. Now, more than ever, that means a tilt in the rules of game toward those who can most easily help candidates meet that test: the better off. The result is a disaster for

Joshua Cohen and Joel Rogers

democracy. As John Rawls explains in his classic essay, "The Basic Liberties and Their Priority" (1982), a basic condition of democracy is that all citizens enjoy a "fair value of political liberty." By giving the wealthy a greater opportunity for political influence, our present system of campaign finance defeats this democratic principle.

What can we do to repair the problem? That question prompts the debate in this New Democracy Forum. Lead authors and campaign finance reform activists David Donnelly, Janice Fine, and Ellen S. Miller think we should finance candidate elections with public money by providing candidates with subsidies on condition that they restrict spending and limit fund-raising from private sources. At the time their piece was published in *Boston Review* (April 1997), the authors were fresh from a ballot initiative victory for this style of reform in Maine (Donnelly managed the campaign); in the November 1998 elections, they registered similar victories in Massachusetts and Arizona.

Respondents Doug Phelps and Zach Polett, by contrast, are veterans of successful campaigns in a number of states that have sought democratic reform by other means: public financing through individual tax credits rather than general revenue allocations, an expanded range of potential recipients of public money (e.g., parties or community or labor organizations), or simply lower limits on acceptable contributions. Respondent

Editors' Preface

Senator Russell Feingold is coauthor (along with Senator John McCain) of the leading reform proposal at the national level—more modest in its depth of reform, obviously more extensive in its potential effect.

At issue among these advocates of different approaches to reform is not the corruption of the present system—that is the common premise—but the best means of achieving meaningful change, the relative importance of getting a level playing field among candidates and ensuring more popular democratic accountability, and trade-offs between more modest and more radical reforms.

Their debate proceeds on shifting ground, and we have seen new developments since this exchange first appeared. The reform proposal passed in Massachusetts differs from the Maine proposal sketched by Donnelly, Fine, and Miller. The latest version of McCain-Feingold—which barely lost in the Senate in 1998, as its counterpart (Shays-Meehan) passed in the House—is not the same as the version discussed here. And in other states and municipalities, other ideas are now being pursued. Still, the contours of the campaign finance problem remain much the same, as do the fundamental ideas about reform strategies outlined here.

Joining the discussion, too, are a number of distinguished academic and "think-tank" students of American politics: Bruce Ackerman, Dan Lowenstein, Tom

Mann, and Josh Rosenkranz. Also joining, in the persons of Steve Rosenthal and Amanda Fuchs, are representatives of "a key player" in those politics—organized labor. The result, we believe, is an unusually hard-hitting, precisely engaged, and practically informed discussion about how to make American democracy live up to its promise.

I

Going Public

DAVID DONNELLY, JANICE FINE,
AND ELLEN S. MILLER

*There are only two important things in politics.
The first is money and I can't remember the second.*
—Mark Hanna

On November 7, 1995, more than a thousand volunteers collected sixty-five thousand signatures to put the Maine Clean Elections Act on that state's 1996 ballot. This was the country's most sweeping campaign finance reform proposal, and it promised to blunt the domination of special-interest money in Maine politics by establishing a system of full public financing of state elections. One year later, by a fifty-six to forty-four margin, Maine voters enacted this fundamental change. In crisp and decisive terms, they stated that private money would no longer dominate their political life.

The situation in other states, however, remains at least as bad as it had been in Maine, and at the federal level matters are much worse. The American people realize that money is eating away at the core of our democracy. Voters seem willing to take decisive action to bring this situation to an end, but they need a model for reform. Maine's full public financing solution, the Clean Money

Option, provides that model—so we will argue. To appreciate the good sense embodied in the Maine solution, we need first to understand the problem and then to appreciate the limits of the alternative solutions.

The Problem

Americans can no longer pick up a newspaper without being confronted with the latest examples of campaign finance excesses—stories about the use of the White House and trade missions for fund-raising purposes, or the invitation of special-interest lobbyists into legislative drafting sessions on Capitol Hill, or Republican legislators vacationing with the largest donors to their party. These stories describe a system gone awry, one in which private money is increasingly driving public policy on an ever wider array of issues, including taxation, environmental regulation, and health care policy, to name just the most obvious. And it is all perfectly legal—or at least, as the president says, 90 percent of it is. The remaining 10 percent—contributions to the Democratic National Committee from well-heeled Asian donors, for example—may be of questionable legality and may create titillating headlines, but it is largely a sideshow (and press coverage is sometimes an ugly, xenophobic sideshow). The real scandal is the legal stuff.

The precise nature of this scandal has been obscured for years by contributors' ingenuity and reformers' lack of information. According to the conventional reading of recent campaign finance history, reform efforts in the early 1970s unwittingly encouraged the formation of political actions committees (PACs), which, by coordinating individual contributions, both multiplied the effects of these contributions and drove up the costs of political campaigning. The big problem, then, was to do something about the PACs.

Skeptical about this conventional wisdom, the Center for Responsive Politics pioneered a system for documenting the thousands of individual contributions to congressional campaigns. As a result of these efforts, we now have a far more accurate picture of the flows of money.[1]

The basic elements of this picture are crystal clear. The total amount of money in the system is rapidly increasing. The vast majority of this money comes from individuals, not PACs, and most individual and PAC contributions come from wealthy special interests with a direct stake in government decisions. Businesses and corporations are becoming increasingly good at targeting their contributions to members of the committees that deal with the issues that affect them (health care corporations target their dollars to members of the health care committees, banking interests target their contributions to members of the banking committees, etc.). And these political investments have sizable payoffs in terms of electoral victories and favorable legislative outcomes.

Consider some basic numbers.

A record $2.2 billion (estimated) was spent in American politics in 1996. About $742.6 million was spent by candidates for Congress. This figure does not include the money that parties and other organizations spent on behalf of candidates. (Common Cause estimates that cost of these "independent expenditures" and "issue advocacy" ads reached $100 million.) In 1996, spending for the presidential election—including the $177 million spent on the primaries—reached $1 billion for the first time.

Overall fund-raising for the Democratic and Republican parties through their federal and non-federal accounts reached $866.1 million through the end of November 1996. The GOP outspent the Democrats $550 million to $315.9 million. The defensive claims from the Democrats about their need to keep up with the Joneses seem somewhat true, but it is hard to feel sorry for the party that also claims to champion the cause of the working class, and they did keep up with the GOP in terms of soft-money contributions—$149.6 million for Republicans and a cool $117.3 million for the Democrats. ("Soft money" refers to the tens or hundreds of thousand-dollar gifts to parties for so-called party-building activities, which invariably come from corporate interests, not working families.)

As to the sources of the money: most political contributions for federal, state, and local election campaigns come from a small number of wealthy individuals and powerful organizations that are subject to government regulation and taxation or have some other stake in government policy making. For example, in the 1996 election cycle less than one-fourth of 1 percent of the American people gave contributions of $200 or more to a federal candidate. Only 4 percent made any contribution of any size to any candidate for office—federal, state, or local. On average, only 20 percent of the money came from individuals giving contributions of less than $200 per candidate. That means that an astonishing 80 percent of political money came from the tiny group of donors who gave $200 or more. (The residents of one New York City zip code gave more to congressional candidates than the residents of each of twenty-four states.)

Funds are intelligently targeted. Recently the timber industry convinced Congress to allow the logging of dead and dying trees on public lands, over the objections of environmental groups. According to the Center for Responsive Politics's *Cashing In Report,* the 54 senators who supported the timber industry had received an average of $20,000 in contributions from industry interests, while the 42 against the idea had received an average of $2,500, and in the House, on average, the 211 members who supported the industry had received $2,500 while the 209 who opposed them had received only $542.

David Donnelly, Janice Fine, and Ellen S. Miller

The military industry also wrote big checks and got big returns. The 213 members of Congress who voted to spend an additional $493 million on Northrop Grumman's B-2 stealth bombers received an average of $2,100 from the contractor; the 210 who voted against only got $100 on average.

With the devolution of important issues, like the implementation of the new welfare laws, to the states, perhaps welfare mothers should start a political action committee or bundle a portion of their dwindling benefits checks to contribute to the reelection efforts of the chairs of the human resource committees in our state capitals. But how many corporate executives need to choose between making a political contribution and buying food for their children?

What does this money buy? *The Nation* has catalogued the "return on investment" that corporate America received in direct corporate welfare from the Commerce Department. Between 1992 and 1994, AT&T contributed $90,000 to the Democrats and received $34.2 million in Commerce Department grants. Boeing gave $127,000 and received $50.9 million from Commerce. General Electric gave $153,000 and got $14.8 million; Shell Petroleum gave $65,000 and got $12 million; and Texaco gave $22,000 got $8.1 million.[2] Nice work if you can get it.

And the money didn't just determine the outcome of

policy debates; it decided races. In 1996 congressional campaigns, the biggest spenders won House races 90 percent of the time and Senate races 80 percent of the time. The Center for Responsive Politics has also determined that in both House and Senate races with no incumbent, candidates who spent the most beat their opponents by a two-to-one ratio. Races in 1996 were not financially competitive—in nearly 40 percent of House races, the winner outspent the loser by a factor of ten to one or more. No candidate who was outspent more than five to one was victorious.

The trends are the same in the states. Maine state politics, for example, has also been dominated by a few wealthy donors and interest groups. Comparable figures—an estimated one half of 1 percent of all voters giving $50 or more to a state candidate—describe the same unlevel playing field for citizens in Maine as exists in national politics. Mainers were persuaded to support campaign finance reform by studies showing an explosion in the cost to run for governor (an increase of 1,609 percent over twenty years) and in targeted special-interest giving to influence policy decisions. When the trucking industry successfully watered down the so-called Tired Truckers bill despite public opinion squarely behind strict enforcement, they did so in part by influence bought with political contributions. When Blue Cross/Blue Shield sought a change in their tax status from not-for-profit to for-profit, a move which could have netted them millions, a study showing their contributions to the Banking and Insurance Committee (released at a "Blues"-sponsored fund-raiser for the committee chair) crystallized public opinion and editorial opposition to the plan, eventually leading to its demise. When the timber industry's favorite incumbent legislator was in trouble in a 1994 reelection fight, paper companies poured $5,000 into the campaign for a last-minute radio spot that proved critical for his six-vote victory. Public outrage about these events was successfully harnessed for a pro-reform effort, culminating in the 1996 election day victory for reformers.

Solutions?

So we have a problem. Simply put, there is too much private money in our political system. Despite the best efforts of a few conservative scholars and columnists, this point is no longer a topic of serious debate. The large question before us is twofold: What role should private money play, and how can we correct the current imbalance? The field is now crowded with competing answers to both parts of the question. To explain the advantages of the Maine strategy over the leading alternatives, we will start by setting out some basic principles that should guide reform efforts, and then we will describe the deficiencies of the alternatives in light of these principles.

Principles

Broad principles should inform any proposal for campaign finance reform. We suggest five:

Competition. Reform must enhance electoral competition. It must encourage qualified Americans of diverse backgrounds and points of view, regardless of their economic means, to seek public office.

Accountability. Reform must increase government accountability and restore public confidence in government. It must eliminate the conflicts of interest created by private financing of the election campaigns of our public officials.

Fairness. Reform must guarantee fairer and more equal representation for all citizens. The views of all citizens must be taken into account in the public policy making process irrespective of their ability to make campaign contributions.

Responsibility. Reform must stop the perpetual money chase. Elected officials should be attending to the people's business—meeting with constituents, attending important meetings, researching current policy options—not lounging with large donors.

Deliberation. Reform must begin the process of reinvigorating public participation in our democracy. It must reinstate public elections and legislative debate as forums for deliberation about how best to address the most pressing issues of the day.

David Donnelly, Janice Fine, and Ellen S. Miller

Alternatives

While it would be impossible to develop an exhaustive list of proposals to address the money in politics problem, six strategies dominate public discussion: lowering campaign contribution limits; raising contribution limits and enhancing disclosure; making lots of modest changes around the edges (like the McCain-Feingold legislation proposed in the Senate); instituting partial public financing or matching funds; challenging the Supreme Court's 1976 *Buckley v. Valeo* decision, which substantially limited the measures that government can use to regulate campaign finance; and full public financing.

Lower contribution limits. A first strategy of reform is to cut into the flow of money as it passes from contributors to candidates—to limit the size of the checks written to candidates for elective office, while not regulating the overall amount of spending. Pursuing this strategy, voters in several states have passed proposals to limit contributions to $100 (or some other level). But these proposals have run into legal trouble. Although the Supreme Court has permitted limits on contributions to candidate campaigns—both because such contributions threaten corruption and because potential contributors remain free to spend their money to influence politics without giving it to specific candidates—the Court confined its concerns to "large" contributions. And lower courts have recently struck down $100 limits in Washington, D.C., Missouri, and Oregon as too stringent and therefore incompatible with First Amendment free speech rights.

Because of these legal decisions, we do not have much experience with more stringent campaign contribution limits. Still, we can make some informed judgments about their effectiveness on the basis of evidence gathered over recent election cycles. Although it appears that the overall amount of money given directly to candidates went down, there was a corresponding increase in "independent expenditures."[3] Moreover, low limits on campaign contributions for individual candidates may have the perverse effect of encouraging candidates to spend even more time courting contributors because a larger number of contributions would be needed to wage a serious campaign. Furthermore, it is and would remain easier for incumbents to find the numbers of contributors needed to mount strong campaigns than it is for challengers to do so. If reduced contribution limits lead to increased independent expenditures, more candidate time on fund-raising, and a playing field that favors incumbents, then such limits do not fare well in terms of the goals of fairness, responsibility, and competitiveness, even if they help on accountability.

Raising contribution limits/more disclosure. A second strategy of reform would put increased weight on full disclosure of support, while raising contribution limits or eliminating them entirely. Pursuing this strategy would, we believe, put the financing of our elections even more securely in the hands of wealthy economic interests and cause an even more dramatic skewing of public policy in favor of the big campaign contributors. Raising the limits would increase the current imbalance in contributions even more. Business interests already contribute seven times as much as labor organizations do, and ten times as much as ideological groups. For example, in 1996, energy interests gave $21 million in congressional races, whereas environmental groups gave just $2 million. As the principles of accountability, fairness, and deliberation imply, the issue isn't simply how much money is being spent and how much time it takes to raise it, but where it comes from, who provides it and who doesn't, and what obligations, commitments, and conflicts of interest result.

At the same time, the remedy of full disclosure falls short. Mere documentation does not correct the imbalances cited above. We already know that economic interests influence, even control the political process. As Congressman Barney Frank (Democrat, Massachusetts) has commented, "We are the only human beings in the world who are expected to take thousands of dollars from perfect strangers on important matters and not be affected by it." Assuming a reliable source of information, disclosure may inform the public of how skewed the process is, but it won't shield our elected officials, nor will it correct for the unfair influence that contributors have over the political process. Like battered women, citizens already know who is hurting them, and how much; they need a way out, not more information about the source and extent of the damage.

Modest changes around the edges. A third strategy aims to control the flow of money—rather than simply providing greater information about it—but differs from contribution limits in the target of the controls. The leading such proposal at the federal level is the McCain-Feingold bill, which includes voluntary spending limits for U.S. Senate candidates, a ban on PAC contributions to candidates for federal office, and regulation of "soft money," and would require federal candidates to rely substantially on in-state contributions. Candidates who agree to the spending limits will receive free television time and reduced postage rates.

Though not without merit, these changes would bring only slight advantages in terms of the reform principles listed above. The voluntary spending limits in McCain-Feingold, for example, are only slightly lower than the current average. The House companion bill (Shays-Meehan) sets these voluntary spending limits higher than the current average amount for House candidates. More fundamentally, though, we would achieve at best limited gains in fairness and accountability. That's because the current problems are not principally a result of PACs or out-of-state state contributions. PACs are now responsible for only 25 percent of funding for congressional campaigns. And because PACs are not the exclusive vehicle for wealthy donors, a PAC ban might further slant the playing field: it would disarm labor unions and other interest groups that raise their money from a large number of small contributions from their members. Business interests do not now rely on PACs for their political contributions. If PACs were banned tomorrow, business would simply channel all, rather than most, of its money through large individual contributions. A PAC ban, if constitutional, would take us back to the days when there were no PACs and most of the money used to finance political campaigns came from wealthy business executives.

Furthermore, the great majority of funds for these races already comes from in state: for senators, 63 percent of their funds came from within their home states, and 78 percent of House candidates' funds were raised from within their home states. Big contributors will continue to have an insurmountable advantage when it comes to gaining access and influence with elected officials; they will just be doing so closer to home.

Partial public financing. The fourth strategy adopts a different angle on reform. Instead of looking for the optimal restrictions on private money, it aims to increase the role of public money as a supplement to private resources, perhaps by using public funds to match small contributions. Although Maine's Clean Elections Act embraces the principle of public financing, we think that alternative schemes of *partial* public financing are worst-of-both-worlds hybrids: they couple the most troubling effects of private financing with the most problematic aspects of public financing.

Consider the best-known case of partial public financing, the system by which we finance our presidential elections. Candidates must first raise lots of special-interest money; after they have become indebted to those private contributors, the candidates then receive their public money. So we are asked to pay twice. First, through public financing, we support presidential candidates who are already obligated to private economic interests; then we finance the tax breaks, subsidies, and other forms of corporate welfare granted to corporate sponsors as paybacks. But even systems of matching funds that (unlike the presidential scheme) attempt to amplify small contributions by providing a high ratio of public money to private money don't change the fundamental calculus because they don't outlaw very large private contributions from wealthy special interests, contributions which, matching funds or no matching funds, are enormously influential.

David Donnelly, Janice Fine, and Ellen S. Miller

Challenging "money equals speech." A fifth line of approach is less a reform strategy in its own right than an effort to set the stage for substantial future reform by challenging the Supreme Court's 1976 decision in *Buckley v. Valeo*. In that case, the Court ruled that political spending was protected by the First Amendment, in effect equating money with speech. Though the Court agreed, as we indicated earlier, that contribution limits are legal, it also held that governments cannot impose overall spending limits on campaigns, or regulate candidates' spending from their own pockets, or limit independent expenditures (money spent by a private group or individual without coordinating with a party or candidate). Because of *Buckley*, there can be no mandatory spending limits and any system of public financing must be optional.

Thus some reformers argue that the first order of business is to challenge Buckley, perhaps through a constitutional amendment that would restrict First Amendment protections of campaign spending. But this cannot be the entire solution to the growing problem of private money in our political system. Even if we could limit spending, we would still have not dealt directly with the corrosive element—the conflicts of interest produced by accepting money from private sources. Moreover, as advocates of the Equal Rights Amendment and the Balanced Budget Amendment would argue, a Constitutional amendment effort takes years and the task of marshaling the forces to ratify it in two-thirds of the states is daunting.

What role *should* private money play in our political system? As our brief sketch of the reform landscape indicates, an answer to this question is central to any assessment of different campaign finance reform proposals. Is contributing money to campaigns an equally legitimate form of participation, alongside voting and volunteering, even though not every American has the means to do it and most do not make contributions? Are large contributions just another form of participation, like going to lots of meetings, or something else altogether? Since all voters are not equally able to make large campaign contributions, how can we square the current system with our egalitarian ideal of "one person, one vote"?

Though Americans accept the legitimacy of the economic inequality that enables the rich to buy fancier cars and more homes, they do not generally accept the current role of private money in our political system because they do not think that the rich are entitled to greater political representation. But the current system establishes precisely that entitlement: it effectively allocates political power according to economic status, and treats participation in the political system just as it treats participation in the marketplace. This is unfair, and the central problem with all the reform proposals we have considered thus far is that they do not do enough to correct this unfairness. To ensure a fair system, in which all citizens have equal opportunities for political influence, we need to look elsewhere.

CLEAN MONEY

Our preferred alternative—which we call the Clean Money Option—is a system of voluntary full public financing that cuts the cord of dependency between candidates and special-interest contributors. While no solution closes off all channels of influence, the Clean Money Option blocks the one that creates the most trouble for the campaign finance reform principles—the donations of large sums of money by special interests to candidates who, should they win, may be able to influence policy on issues of importance to these donors. This is the proposal that Maine voters have enacted and that legislatures and citizens in Vermont, Connecticut, North Carolina, Illinois, Massachusetts, Missouri, Idaho, Washington, and Wisconsin (for example) will consider in the coming months and years.

The law that Maine voters passed was based on model legislation concerning federal elections that was drafted by the Working Group on Electoral Democracy in the late 1980s.[4] This proposal called for full public financing of campaigns for candidates who agree to spending limits, no private money, and a shorter campaign season. Over the course of several years, Maine activists rewrote this model to fit the political realities of running for office in Maine, and those of running a statewide referendum campaign to pass the legislation.

The Maine Clean Elections Act was drafted to go as far as possible in the public financing direction while remaining within the confines of Buckley. The construction of the act makes as many changes as possible on the private side and it creates a public financing option. The measure sets lower, but not overly restrictive, contribution limits for candidates who continue to exercise their right to privately finance their campaigns, and, at its center, it establishes the "Clean Elections Option" to publicly finance candidates who agree to spending limits and to neither seek nor spend any private money.

For the first time, office seekers will have the option of qualifying for and accepting only public money for their election campaigns. Here is how it works.

Candidates who choose to enter into the Clean Elections Option and accept public money must agree to limit their campaign spending to the amount provided in public money and to refuse all private contributions once the public money comes in. They must also agree to a shorter campaign season. These candidates don't get something for nothing. To qualify for public funds, they must collect a specified number of $5 qualifying contributions from voters in their district (or the entire state, in the case of those running for governor or other statewide office). A small amount of private money can be raised as start-up funds or "seed money," but these contributions are limited to $100 per donor and there is an overall cap on the total. The key difference between this system and matching funds schemes is that under the Clean Elections Option, candidates can neither raise nor spend any private money once they receive public money. Moreover, this law covers primaries as well as general elections. Clean Election candidates would also receive supplementary public funds if they were outspent by privately financed opponents, or by independent expenditures, or a by combination of the two. These funds would be capped at twice the original amount provided to the candidate.

Returning to our five principles, what are the advantages of the Clean Money option? By providing an alternative to the special interest–driven system for financing elections, the Clean Money Option will level the playing field for candidates, thus enhancing electoral competition. At the same time, it will lower the economic barriers now faced by citizens who might consider running for office and, by reducing the role of private money, it will increase the importance of those political activities that are available to all citizens. In both ways, the Clean Money Option should mean a fairer political system, with greater equality in opportunities for political influence. Unlike any other proposals, the Clean Money Option also strengthens accountability by eliminating political contributions as a way of influencing legislative deliberation and policy making. In addition, the Clean Money Option would encourage responsibility by freeing our elected officials from the perpetual money chase and allowing them to use their time to engage important issues of the day free of the undue influence of special-interest money. Finally, while the implications of this system for political deliberation remain uncertain, the same can be said for any of the other proposals, and there is no reason to think that public financing will produce greater distractions from important public issues than the current system does.

Politics

When Maine reformers first raised the possibility of a public financing system, they were told they were dreaming, that voters would never go for public financing. And with politicians like President Clinton urging that we squeeze politics into bite-sized morsels, proposing a total overhaul of the way we pay for elections seemed quixotic. But Maine voters countered the prevailing wisdom and passed the proposal by a convincing margin.

Why was this case different? For three reasons.

First, and most straightforwardly, partial measures

and tinkering around the edges are ineffective, and the American public knows it.

Second, people are so disgusted with the current role of money in politics that they are willing to entertain fundamental changes in the rules of the game. Polling results consistently show that issue of campaign finance lies at the heart of citizen discontent with politics. Americans believe that Washington's failure to address their problems is the direct result of politicians accepting too much campaign money from special interests. They believe that politicians must now bow to the agendas of those who sign the checks.

Public opinion is way ahead of politicians on the public financing solution. Polling by the Mellman Group (for the Center for Responsive Politics) shows that Americans are now more supportive of a public financing solution to the problems of money and politics than at any time since Watergate. Gallup polling done before the recent revelations about campaign finances in Washington showed support for public financing equal to that seen in the mid-1970s. A national poll done for Citizen Action by Stanley Greenberg showed that 61 percent of those polled support "a new law where the federal government would provide a fixed amount of money for the campaigns for Congress and all private contributions would be prohibited."

Other recent studies and public opinion research corroborates these findings. The League of Women Voters and the Harwood Group conducted a series of longitudinal focus groups/discussions with citizens in six cities across the country. The participants concluded that a system that provides an option for keeping all special-interest money out and replacing it with public money was needed as one step toward restoring faith in the democratic process. Five separate statewide polls conducted by Bannon Research in 1994 revealed similar sentiments.

But, as political junkies like to say, the only poll that matters is taken on election day. And here we come to the third factor: elections are won by organizations. And the Maine campaign provides instructive lessons for other efforts elsewhere.

The campaign waged by Maine Voters for Clean Elections was a result of years of research, coalition building, and grassroots organizing. With ongoing technical assistance from the Northeast Citizen Action Resource Center (a regional network of progressive organizations and elected leaders), a group of Maine reformers identified the problem, established a role for their analysis in the public dialogue, and became the arbiters of what was—and was not—serious reform. Building a reputation for fair and nonpartisan research, the Maine reformers reached out to all parts of the political spectrum to build the basic coalition necessary to move the issue forward. Coalition partners—including the state chapters of the League of Women Voters, the American Association of Retired People, Common Cause, the Maine AFL-CIO, leading environmental and women's organizations, the Citizen Action affiliate, and the Perot-led Reform Party—met for two and a half years to draft a solution that would withstand constitutional challenge, effectively address the problem, and be politically viable. The idea was to be principled and to win.

When the coalition could not move principled reform through the Maine state legislature (forty reform bills, some good, most bad, died in the state legislature over a period of ten years), its members, under the banner Maine Voters for Clean Elections, decided to bring the issue directly to the voters. Through a substantial grassroots effort, the coalition collected sixty-five thousand signatures in a single day (as we noted at the beginning of this essay) to place a binding referendum question on the 1996 ballot. Demonstrating the breadth of its appeal, the campaign recruited business leaders and received the active endorsement of the former director of the state's Chamber of Commerce as well as that of a well-respected former CEO of the Bath Iron Works, the largest private employer in the state.

An aggressive public education campaign—waged door-to-door, at forums, in the media, and on the airwaves—ensued, with the aim of persuading Maine voters to adopt, in the language of the ballot question, "new campaign laws and give public funding for state candidates who agree to spending limits." By mid-summer, the initiative had the support of a plurality but not a majority of voters. The large hurdle was the public financing strategy itself: though a substantial majority supported the results that public financing would produce —blunting the influence of special interests and leveling the playing field for candidates—many had trouble believing that the system could in fact be cleaned up and many were especially hesitant about public financing (historically unpopular) as a means for advancing these goals. To counter these doubts, the reformers framed the argument in terms of problems and goals, rather than means: "What will Question 3 do? It will lower campaign spending by providing a Clean Elections Option of public money for candidates who agree not to take any private special interest money." Their public education efforts struck a similar balance between the problem and the proposed solution; for example, in the last eight weeks of the campaign, two hundred supporters submitted letters to the editor to various newspapers each week, alternating between discussing the problem and explaining the solution.

In short, Maine Voters for Clean Elections organized a broad coalition extending well beyond the "usual suspects," spoke directly to citizens in countless forums and meetings, and kept an emphasis on the goals of reform, not simply the means. There are no formulas for political success, but reformers elsewhere might use these features of the Maine experience as instructive benchmarks.

Conclusion

Can the Maine law be generalized to the federal level? A Clean Money Option will certainly face rough sledding in Washington, but so will all other serious reforms. Moreover, tangible signs suggest that Maine's success story is not falling on deaf ears. A number of U.S. senators are poised to introduce a Clean Money Option bill in Congress, which would at once signify progress and provide the opportunity for those of us who care about this approach to enter the national debate.

But the most dramatic and immediate impact of Maine's success will be felt in other states, at the state level. Nearly a dozen states have some kind of full public financing proposal under legislative consideration or headed for the ballot. Editorial endorsements have come from all over, from national, regional, and local papers, including *USA Today*, the *Boston Globe*, the *St. Louis Post-Dispatch*, the *Hartford Courant*, the *Rutland Herald* (Vermont), and the *Portland Press Herald* (Maine). The Boston Globe wrote that the Maine plan ought to be considered a "blueprint" for national reform.

While the near-term focus for debate on campaign finance reform will be in Washington, D.C., the real debate about the appropriate role of private money in our public elections and public policy forums will take place in the states. Inside the Beltway the dominant question is, What can be won today? We should be asking, What is worth winning? Keeping that question in focus is the goal of a new national education effort spearheaded by a new Washington, D.C.–based national organization, Public Campaign. This group is working to galvanize broad public support behind reforms that fully address the central and most egregious aspect of today's campaign finance system—the direct financing of our public officials by private interests. And, in due course, the old adage from Downeast may once again come alive: "As Maine goes, so goes the nation."

Postscript

Since we wrote this piece, in early 1997, much has happened to advance the cause of Clean Money. In late spring of 1997, in response to strong public pressure, the Vermont state legislature enacted a comprehensive package of reforms similar to the Maine initiative. On election day 1998, two more states joined the Clean Money fold. After a vigorous fifteen-month campaign involving ix thousand citizen activists, Massachusetts voters passed the initiative by a two-to-one margin. By a slimmer margin Arizona became the first Western state to enact Clean Money reform. Several *New York Times* editorials singled out these efforts as promising new developments in the struggle to enact meaningful campaign finance reform.

At the national level, reformers came closer than ever before to passing moderate reform but were stymied by special interests and a Senate out of touch with public concerns. Indeed, September 1998 polling done by Public Campaign in eight states demonstrated that Americans were willing to support the most far reaching reforms placed before them. At the same time, Senators John Kerry and Paul Wellstone and Representative John Tierney have introduced legislation modeled after the victorious state Clean Money initiatives. Sadly, however, in November of 1998 the Supreme Court declined the opportunity to revisit the *Buckley* decision in a case originating in Cincinnati, where the city council had imposed mandatory spending limits.

We continue to believe that the real scandal in our political system is what is legal, and that only reforms like those passed in Maine, Vermont, Massachusetts, and Arizona will result in significant change. We are emboldened by the growing ranks of activists and organizations in forty states who share this vision, and we look forward to adding a good number of those forty to the list of Clean Money states when this book goes into its second printing.

II

Modest Reform?

SENATOR RUSSELL FEINGOLD
(DEMOCRAT, WISCONSIN)

𝒟onnelly, Fine, and Miller's critique of S.25, the McCain-Feingold campaign finance reform bill, is by now familiar—I might say well worn—and it misses the mark just as widely as it did the first time it was raised.

The general thrust of this critique is that only a concerted effort to enact a system of public financing of political campaigns will cure the many ills of our corrupt system, and that efforts to enact legislation like our bill are wasted because we are offering only "modest changes around the edges" rather than substantial reform. Even allowing for possible differences in the definition of the word "modest," this critique is misleading at best.

As the basis for this erroneous assertion of modesty, the authors address only parts of McCain-Feingold: the restriction on contributions from political action committees (PACs), the requirement that candidates who wish to qualify for limited free television time and other benefits raise at least 60 percent of their campaign funds from individuals in their home states, and the voluntary spending limit. Their critique does not, however, discuss the most significant provision in the bill, the ban on so-called soft-money contributions.

Unregulated and unlimited by federal law, soft-money contributions represent the worst example of the excesses and corrupting nature of the current system of financing political campaigns, and the sums being contributed have grown rapidly. According to a January 10, 1997, Federal Election Commission report, cited in a recent Congressional Research Service analysis, Republican national committees raised about $141 million for their soft-money accounts from January 1, 1995, to November 25, 1996, an increase of 183 percent over the same time period in the 1991–92 election cycle, and Democratic national committees raised about $122 million during this same period, a 217 percent jump from the amount raised during the 1991–92 election cycle.

Soft-money contributions do not come from average Americans but from the wealthiest sectors of our society. This in turn enhances the influence of the wealthy few over the political process and contributes to the erosion of the one-person/one-vote principle on which our electoral system is based. Shutting down the channel for $263 million's worth of soft-money contributions is no "modest" change.

Donnelly, Fine, and Miller do touch on the other major provision of McCain-Feingold, the benefits granted to candidates who adhere to voluntary spending limits, but they fail to appreciate its significance. Candidates

Modest Reform?

who agree to voluntarily limit their campaign spending would be eligible to receive thirty minutes of free television time during the general election period, and they would receive additional discounted television time and a discount on postage rates for campaign mailings.

To receive these benefits, candidates must voluntarily agree to three limitations on campaign spending:

- They must agree voluntarily to limit their spending following guidelines that would be based upon a state's voting-age population. Less populous states like Vermont or Utah, for example, would have a general election spending limit of just under $1 million, while the limit for general election spending in California would rise to about $5.5 million.
- They must voluntarily agree to limit the amount of personal funds spent on behalf of their candidacies. This limit would be $250,000, or 10 percent of the general election spending limit in a particular state, whichever is less. In my home state of Wisconsin, for example, the personal spending limit would be about $150,000.
- They must voluntarily agree to raise 60 percent of their overall campaign funds from individuals within their home states.

By lowering spending—voluntarily—we reduce the cost of campaigns and take some of the pressure off candidates to raise large sums of money. By requiring candidates to raise most of their money at home, we get them to focus on the people they wish to represent.

Donnelly, Fine, and Miller claim that this provision too amounts to only a modest change, but the analysis on which they base this dismissive opinion is flawed.

First, they state that "the voluntary spending limits in McCain-Feingold ... are only slightly lower than the current average." Since the voluntary spending limits in our bill would differ from state to state, I don't see how an "average" figure means much for purposes of comparison.

Let's take a couple of examples. Under the voluntary limits provision of McCain-Feingold, the highest amount anyone running for the United States Senate in California could spend would be $5.5 million in the general election and $8.25 million overall. During the last Senate race there, in 1994, Republican Michael Huffington spent nearly $30 million and Democrat Dianne Feinstein spent more than $14 million. An $8.25 million overall voluntary spending cap would, of course, have resulted in greatly lower expenditures.

During the 1996 Senate race in Massachusetts, Democrat John Kerry spent about $8.8 million and Republican William Weld spent almost $6 million. The $3 million overall voluntary spending limit under McCain-Feingold would have substantially reduced the cost of that race as well.

Modest Reform?

I would add that an analysis prepared by Public Citizen found that nearly 75 percent of the current members of the U.S. Senate spent more on their most recent campaigns than they would be allowed to spend under the voluntary restrictions included in McCain-Feingold. That is meaningful change.

Donnelly, Fine, and Miller also downplay our requirement that candidates raise 60 percent of their overall funds from individuals within their home states. The authors state that "the great majority of funds for these races already come from in state: for senators, 63 percent of their funds come from within their home states, and 78 percent of House candidates' funds were raised from within their home states."

This assertion is based upon the analysis of the 1994 elections done by the Center for Responsive Politics (CRP), which looked at individual contributions of $200 or more. CRP's figures did not include PAC money or small contributions. In that analysis, twenty of thirty-five senators elected in 1994 raised at least 60 percent of their funds that came from that fund-raising sector (individual contributions of at least $200) from within their own states. But that sector, according to CRP, accounted for only 41 percent of all campaign funds raised by Senate incumbents during 1994. Our bill reaches more broadly; it requires that at least 60 percent of a candidate's *entire* fund-raising come from individuals within the candidate's home state. That is a larger universe than the one used by the CRP study. So the proposed reform would amount to a more significant change in the current system than Donnelly, Fine, and Miller assert.

The authors also disparage the restrictions on PAC contributions in our bill, claiming that these restrictions "would disarm labor unions and other interest groups" and not touch business interests. Our PAC restrictions are not the centerpiece of this bill—the soft-money ban and the voluntary spending limits are—and the PAC restrictions provision, which is currently under negotiation, must be considered with the other parts of our bill.

I think it's safe to say that all of us who are working so hard to reform the campaign finance system agree about the extent and the gravity of the problem we face and the need for genuine, fundamental reform. The McCain-Feingold bill, the first bipartisan campaign finance reform legislation introduced in the U.S. Senate in more than a decade, is one avenue to reform. It is not a perfect bill, in fact, it is not my ideal bill. I have authored public finance legislation in the 104th and 105th Congresses, but, frankly, given the political dynamics in Congress (Democrats and Republicans have had a long-standing philosophical divide over the merits of public financing), I am not optimistic about the chances for success. In fact, Donnelly, Fine, and Miller acknowledge that the coalition that eventually got the Maine Clean Election Act passed by referendum "could not move principled reform

Modest Reform?

through the Maine state legislature." It would be no easier in Congress.

McCain-Feingold is a strong, positive step towards genuine reform. It has broad support from organizations like Common Cause, Public Citizen, the Reform Party, and the American Association of Retired Persons. It has bipartisan support in the Senate. It eliminates $400,000 in soft-money contributions and, for the first time, provides challengers with the tools to run competitive campaigns against well-entrenched incumbents. It helps return the focus of the campaign to the voters and helps free candidates from the money chase. That is far more than "modest" reform.

Reform of our political system will not come in one dramatic stroke, but by patient work and deliberate process. Since we are all working hard to reform that system, let's continue to work together.

Postscript

This article was originally written to respond to criticisms of the version of the McCain-Feingold bill that was introduced in the Senate in early 1997. As Ellen Miller and her colleagues point out in their postscript, much has happened to campaign finance reform since then. Most important, from the point of view of the issues discussed in this article, is that Senator McCain and I decided to modify our bill before pressing for its consideration on the floor of the Senate. We did that to increase our chances of gaining Republican support for the bill.

The version of the McCain-Feingold bill considered by the Senate and blocked by a filibuster in September 1997, and again in February and September 1998, does not include voluntary spending limits or limitations on PACs or out-of-state contributions. Instead, it deals primarily with two major problems in our current campaign finance system that do not directly touch on candidate spending or fund-raising—soft money and phony-issue ads. Ellen Miller and the organization she heads, Public Campaign, supported the revised version of our bill.

Indeed, the reforms contained in the McCain-Feingold bill, moderate and incremental though they may be, have the support of the entire reform community. That unanimous support played a significant role in the successful effort to pass reform in the House of Representatives in the summer of 1998. The Shays-Meehan bill, modeled on the modified version of McCain-Feingold, passed the House by a convincing bipartisan vote on August 6, 1998.

In light of the House action on the Shays-Meehan bill and the 1998 elections, which showed in a number of ways the public's strong desire for campaign finance reform, Senator McCain and I intend to continue our work in the next Congress for moderate bipartisan reform. There are obviously different views on the best

Modest Reform?

strategy for achieving meaningful reform, and the submissions to this forum are very useful in illustrating the factors that those of us who work in the legislative arena must weigh in reaching our decision on what course to follow. I do believe, however, and I hope that the others who participated in this discussion will agree, that all of us must work together if we are to succeed in passing reform to improve the health of our democracy and restore public confidence in the Congress.

Empower Citizens

ZACH POLETT

On the same day that 313,581 Maine voters were passing the Maine Clean Elections Act by a 56 to 44 percent margin, 487,432 Arkansas voters were passing the Arkansas Clean Government Act by nearly double that margin—66 percent to 34 percent—a greater margin, in fact, than that by which they supported native son Bill Clinton's reelection as president.

We at ACORN (the Association of Community Organizations for Reform Now) applaud the work of our sisters and brothers in New England in passing what we agree is significant campaign finance reform in Maine. But we are surprised that Donnelly, Fine, and Miller neglect the innovative tax credit public financing reform measure passed in Arkansas that we believe also serves as a valuable model for serious campaign finance reform in the years to come, either in combination with state-run "Clean Money" elections funds or by itself.

The Arkansas initiative accomplishes the following:

1. *Contribution Limits.* Reduces the $1,000 contribution limit per candidate per election to $300 for statewide office and $100 for other offices.

Empower Citizens

2. *Tax Credit Public Financing.* Provides public financing by allowing a 100 percent annual tax credit of $50 for individuals and $100 for married couples for contributions to a candidate committee, a political party, or a political committee.

3. *Small-Donor PACs.* Sets up a new class of committees that may receive no more than $25 from any contributor but may contribute up to $2,500 to a candidate.

4. *Independent Expenditure Committees.* Requires disclosure of the contributions these committees receive and limits these contributions to $500 per contributor.

5. *Disclosure.* Tightens disclosure requirements to $50 for candidates and, for the first time in Arkansas history, requires the disclosure of contributions to political parties.

6. *Local Government.* Allows local governments to enact their own stricter campaign finance laws.

In the first few months since the passage of the Arkansas Clean Government Act, we have already seen results. Republican Governor Mike Huckabee had to cut back his gala December 1996 $1,000-per-plate fundraiser to accommodate the new $300 limit. Candidates who played under the new rules in a January 1997 special legislative election reported to the local press that they spent much more time in door-to-door campaigning because "the new rule lessens lobbyist influence and makes the process more accessible to average people." And the city of Little Rock has introduced and is likely to pass a New Party–sponsored ordinance, made possible by the new state law, that severely restricts when city council members can fund-raise, thus helping to reduce conflicts of interest.

The Need for Accountability

As the campaign finance reform community moves forward in its efforts to fundamentally change the financing system of American politics, we think it's important to develop a system that encourages and empowers everyday voters to organize and participate in the process and thus increases the accountability of candidates and politicians to organized groups of voters. We believe that politics in America is already too candidate-centered, as opposed to being issues- or values-centered. We certainly want a system that decreases the dependence of politicians on wealthy individuals and well-financed corporate interests, but not by strengthening the power of politicians and weakening that of organized groups of "regular" voters.

As we often say in the campaign finance reform movement, "Follow the money." We are concerned that if we create a campaign financing system that provides public money to politicians but not to organized groups of citizens, then we will inadvertently create a system that encourages candidates and elected officials to be even less accountable than they are now. If candidates get all their legal political money straight from the government, they will have the funds to speak more and listen less.

If public funding goes only to candidates and all other money is kept out of the process, then candidates will be greatly empowered vis-à-vis voters. We're not convinced that this is such a good thing.

As we change the campaign finance system in America, we want to change who it is that the politicians have to listen to, but we don't want to make them independent actors who don't need to listen to anyone except the pollsters. Therefore, as we develop public funding mechanisms for political campaigns, we need to make sure that all the cash doesn't go directly to candidates.

Tax Credits as a Public Financing Tool

The Arkansas initiative uses tax credits as its public financing tool. The way it works is that every Arkansan effectively has $50 of political public financing dollars from the state government ($100 for a married couple) that he or she can allocate as he or she deems fit. Individuals can direct their pieces of public financing to a candidate, to a political party, or to a political committee. Voters can send it all to one, or divide it up any way they choose. They can invest their piece of public financing in a candidate's campaign or in a political group with which they agree. They can even decide not to invest it at all—in which case the state, not the individual, keeps the money.

The mechanism for this contribution is that individuals make the contribution or contributions and then get the funds back from the state as a dollar-for-dollar reduction of their state income tax bill or as an addition to their annual state income tax refund.

Candidates, parties, and organized groups (political committees) will thus compete with each other for these public funds by working to convince voters that they should direct their share of public financing in that candidate's or that group's direction. All Arkansans will be equal in this process, since all will have the same $50 to allocate. And non-Arkansans will not be able to make an allocation since they are not Arkansas taxpayers.

Small-Donor Political Action Committees

The Arkansas initiative sets up and defines a new kind of political action committee called a "small-donor political action committee." These committees are restricted to accepting small contributions of no more than $25 from each individual. Thus they are nearly equally accessible to "lean cats" as they are to "fat cats"—and the fat cats' contributions need to be pretty lean, no more than $25.

What makes the small-donor PAC particularly effective as a campaign finance reform tool is its interaction with the contribution limits of the initiative. Under the initiative, regular PACs and individuals can contribute no more than $100 per election to a candidate (or $300 for a statewide race), while small-donor PACs are allowed to contribute up to $2,500. Thus small-donor PACs empower small donors while decreasing the power of traditional, large-donor PACs. They also have the advantage of putting more money into the system, thus answering one of the objections raised to relatively low contribution limits.

Reality Check

Let's be real. The rich and powerful, both corporations and individuals, will always have more political influence than the rest of us, especially those of us who are poor. Money talks. The Maine and Arkansas initiatives, for example, don't restrict private money expenditures by, or contributions to, "independent expenditure" campaigns or political parties. No campaign finance reform law can ever totally level the playing field—not in Maine, not in Arkansas, not through a constitutional amendment. But we don't need to oversell the reforms we're promoting. The current system is broken and everyone knows it. The best we can do is to change the rules of the game in ways that help empower voters and promote candidate accountability, while decreasing somewhat the overriding influence of wealthy contributors.

The authors of "Going Public" are on target when they state that "the real scandal is the legal stuff," not what's illegal, but they miss an important part of the picture when they claim that the problem is private money financing our public elections. The problem is not the private money *per se*, but the vast inequality of who has this private money—primarily large corporations and wealthy individuals.

As the campaign finance reform community evaluates strategy for the next several years, we think that it should look seriously at strategies in a number of states, like those enacted by Arkansas voters in 1996, that are designed to increase and empower organized groups of everyday voters. Tax credit public financing and small-donor political action committees are two important tools to keep in our arsenal.

Setting Limits

DOUGLAS PHELPS

There is no one correct strategy to win campaign finance reform.

The publicly financed clean elections strategy is one approach. A "low-limits" strategy is another. This second route sets tough low limits on the size of contributions, on out-of-district contributions, and on spending, coupling these limits with tax credits for small contributions and liberal allowances for "people PACs" (those which take only very small donations of $25 or less).

Proponents of these two strategies have much in common—a grassroots perspective, a shared focus on the wholesale corruption of the system, and an antipathy toward the flawed McCain-Feingold legislation, which would actually *raise* existing campaign contribution limits.[1] We must work supportively.

But we must also debate the relative advantages of different strategies as we proceed to test and refine them.

If proving our commitment to principled reform were the only goal, the flag of public financing would provide glorious colors under which to soldier forth. But since winning the battle is paramount, it may be the wrong flag to hoist.

Why? Because the low-limits strategy frames the problem more cogently, appeals to voters, and generates a popular outcry against the Supreme Court's twisted anti-reform logic.

Framing the Problem

The first challenge for reformers is to properly frame the campaign finance problem: the fact that moneyed special interests exercise absolute control over election outcomes, and over the politicians who get elected, via campaign contributions.[2] And we need to name the enemy —the rich people and corporations who have bought government lock, stock, and barrel.[3]

There is a lot of noise out in the popular culture about what is wrong with campaign financing. Most of it misleads. The problem is *not* that there is too much money in politics. Were campaign spending devoted to informative dialogue on the issues facing America, rather than negative thirty-second TV spots, would we not welcome *more* money in politics, rather than less? Newt Gingrich is right—it *is* a little pathetic that we spend less as a society on political debate than we do on yogurt or toothpaste. The public is offended by the amount of meaningless negative advertising, not the amount of spending *per se.*

Nor is the basic problem that politicians spend too much time raising campaign money. To be sure, fundraising reduces the time that elected officials spend on more important duties. But this problem is incidental—not the fundamental issue.

The problem is also not that citizens attempt to influence who gets elected using every means allowed, which today includes donations. This is what a democracy is all about; the more the citizenry is engaged in trying to influence the outcome of elections, the healthier the democracy.

Nor is the problem that citizens attempt to get access to politicians, or ask before voting or working for a candidate what they can expect from the candidate in return. Voters should be vigilant and organize to hold politicians accountable, and politicians should listen to voters. It is true that when a politician casts a vote on an issue with a particular, economically self-interested donor agitating in the wings, any quid pro quo involved crosses an important line. But whether or not such behavior sinks to the level of actual corruption is mostly a matter of the timing of the vote, the manner of the contribution, and the explicitness of the bargain. The excesses at the margins of everyday political fundraising—the ones that make headlines—are little more than boneheaded pratfalls along a path which all candidates and big donors routinely travel in a more artful and "law-abiding" manner.

Imagine, for a moment, a new electoral system in which donors could not meet with candidates or lobby them, in which donations would have to be anonymously given through an FEC fund established for this purpose but would continue to be earmarked for the candidate of the donor's choice. The campaign finance "problems" referred to above would be largely eliminated, but the same candidates would keep attracting the big money and getting elected. The process would be "clean," but the bias in government toward the moneyed interests would remain.

So what is the *real* problem? Simply this: If electoral outcomes in a modern mass-communication society are largely determined by the amount of money spent on campaigning,[4] and private money is the source of campaign funding, and the wealthy (and special interests) are allowed to give contributions of a size which are beyond the reach of average citizens, such that politicians raise virtually all of their money from these large contributors[5]—then it inevitably follows that successful candidates will be those whose ideas and positions appeal to the wealthy and to moneyed special interests. Candidates with such appeal will raise the most money, and they will win. And because candidates do not run to lose, politicians and the political parties will look increasingly alike on all issues, at least those of importance to moneyed interests.

Welcome to the present.[6] Since the advent of television in the early 1950s and the rise of a Madison Avenue approach to marketing political candidates, the value of big money to politicians has grown steadily, and the dominance of big money over politics is now virtually complete. This *wholesale* corruption of the democracy, characterized by the dependence of *all* candidates on wealthy donors to finance TV advertising, is what is new in American politics. The *retail* corruption—influence-peddling and the quid pro quo—is no more prevalent than it was in prior eras, and perhaps less so, given the watchful eye of the broadcast news media, bans on taking gifts, and the replacement of the smoke-filled room with the primary system for nominating candidates.

A merit of the public financing solution is that it addresses the real problem. From a policy perspective, it appeals. But from an organizing perspective—the need to frame the problem simply and to name the enemy—it is not so attractive. As it most naturally translates in an average citizen's mind—"using my tax dollars to finance politicians' campaigns"—public financing does not intuitively connect to the problem. It requires too much context and explanation.

In contrast, the contribution limits strategy—"limit what rich people can donate so that it's closer to an amount ordinary people can contemplate"—makes more immediate sense. This strategy directly puts the problem on our terms, that is, that rich people have an unfair advantage over the rest of us.

From an organizing point of view, the limits strategy frames the problem and names the enemy more clearly than does a public financing strategy.

Winning

What about the important question of popular appeal and winning?

The success of the 1996 Maine ballot initiative on public financing notwithstanding,[7] today's voters hate taxes, distrust politicians, and deplore campaign spending in its current form. It is an uphill challenge to persuade them to give their tax dollars to politicians to finance more negative TV spots: "I don't want my taxes being raised, I don't want politicians on the dole, and I'm sick of these thirty-second political ads. Why would I want public financing?"

Add to that the persuasive libertarian objection that politicians will abuse public financing to manipulate elections. According to this argument, we should not establish a system whereby those who govern have the power to tax the governed and use the money to finance their own campaigns, with rules established by themselves. Abuse of such power is inevitable and happens routinely in other nations.

Indeed, it is already happening here. Public financing for presidential campaigns is rigged to prevent anyone

Setting Limits

but billionaires from challenging the two dominant political parties. Were this system used in Russia, for example, with two parties getting over $150 million in public money and all other parties and candidates required to obtain 5 percent of the vote *first* before qualifying for *any* money in *future* elections, it would be ridiculed as a throwback to the old totalitarian ways.

From a policy standpoint, *fair* public financing of elections would achieve laudable results and clean elections. But from an organizing standpoint, it is a strategy highly vulnerable to attack: "Foodstamps for politicians!" In Maine, the public financing initiative passed with an unusually well-funded campaign behind it and little opposition ever mounted. Voters presumably saw it as simply a referendum against "special money in politics." Even so, it received a much smaller percentage of the vote than winning low-limits initiatives have gotten.[8]

And one must wonder whether, once a public financing system is in place, demagogues will emerge to horrify voters by characterizing it as "your tax dollars being wasted on all this negative mudslinging on TV!" If public financing is the norm and nothing is done simultaneously to curtail the negative TV ads that tax dollars will subsidize, the outcry could be enormous, and the search begun for "whoever came up with the idea for this incredible boondoggle."

Clearly, the success in Maine should be followed up elsewhere. But perhaps a more publicly palatable form of the clean election model should be readied, using tax credits (as did ACORN's winning initiative in Arkansas) or vouchers for small contributions, or matching funds, and/or simply by providing free TV and radio time and mailing privileges to candidates.

In the meantime, the low-limits strategy, supported by huge voter majorities at the polls in Missouri, Montana, Oregon, Colorado, the District of Columbia, Arkansas, and California,[9] should be pushed: limit contributions to a size within the reach of average citizens, such as a maximum of $100, so everyone is on a more level playing field when it comes to participating in politics; limit the amount of money a candidate can accept from outside his or her district to (say) no more than 25 percent of total fund-raising, thereby forcing reliance on support from constituents entitled to vote for a candidate; limit spending (including independent and personal expenditures) to low levels that allow candidates who do not depend on large contributions to nonetheless raise sufficient money to compete; and severely limit big-money PACs while empowering people PACs, which take only very small donations.

Voters have repeatedly supported such ideas in recent years at the ballot box. Indeed, the campaign finance cause has been resuscitated largely because of these victories. Earlier strategies, which failed to get traction for over twenty years, starting in the late 1970s, emphasized public financing and congressional action. Momentum behind campaign finance reform was generated by dropping public financing as an issue and taking the case to the people, at the state and local level, in ballot initiatives.

If we want to win, shouldn't we be cautious in hauling the old baggage back on board?

CHALLENGING THE SUPREME COURT

Obviously, the low-limits strategy must place increased emphasis on the need for a constitutional amendment, unless public interest lawyers are able to engineer an overturning of *Buckley v. Valeo*. (Indeed, any successful reform, including public financing, requires either a constitutional amendment or a Supreme Court reversal to deal with the problems of independent expenditures and the wealthy self-financed candidate.)

In *Buckley*, the Supreme Court began by equating the act of spending money to promote speech with speech itself, and concluded that political spending and contributions are protected by the First Amendment. That view is wrong.

Each citizen has one voice, and freeing all those voices from government imposition serves various "social goods." Moreover, the First Amendment protects each voice equally, and that is fundamentally democratic. But money is neither free nor equal. To provide paid-for speech the same protection as simple speech is insidiously undemocratic.

The fundamental argument of grassroots reformers must be that a correct reading of the First Amendment does not forbid any limits whatsoever which the sovereign people may wish to place on campaign spending or contributions, so long as they apply equally and fairly to everyone.[10]

A central aspiration of the Bill of Rights was to protect the powerless from the abuse of concentrated power. The Bill of Rights, properly understood, is not a bar to reform, it is a clarion call for reform. "Get special-interest money out of politics!" is today the moral equivalent of "Don't tread on me!" some two hundred years ago.

The whole idea of the First Amendment was to guarantee that everyone's voice would be heard. The Court's current reasoning in *Buckley* elevates the voice of the wealthy few and drowns out the voice of the many—of ordinary citizens. It should be reversed.

But if the Supreme Court does not reverse itself, then we need a constitutional amendment to allow any limits which the people or their representatives may wish to place on campaign spending and contributions, including so-called independent expenditures, soft money, and/or a candidate's spending from personal wealth.[11]

Such an amendment should not be a cause of great

Setting Limits

worry among reformers. It is illogical to argue that the First Amendment does not apply to campaign spending and contributions but that making this point explicit within the text of the Constitution is "amending the First Amendment" and is thus too scary to contemplate.

A new amendment would merely clarify the First Amendment for federal judges, spelling out clearly what is already evident and commonsensical to the voters of America.[12] Namely, that the control of big money over politics kills democracy and must be ended.

Get special-interest money out of politics. Don't tread on us.

Clean and Constitutional

E. JOSHUA ROSENKRANZ

Measures to reform the way we finance political campaigns are dropping like flies. *Buckley v. Valeo*, the landmark U.S. Supreme Court case that dominates the field of campaign finance reform, has been invoked by courts at all levels to frustrate popular reforms of every flavor. *Buckley* has almost come to stand for the proposition that if it's effective, it must be unconstitutional. As Donnelly, Fine, and Miller indicate, voters seem willing to take decisive action if only the courts will let them do it. But that's a big "if."

Consider the record. Scores of promising reforms that have been enacted into law have fallen to a *Buckley* challenge. And every reform that voters have passed by initiative on election day—in Arkansas, California, Colorado, Montana, and even in Maine—is currently besieged by litigation. Given this record, it is natural to be skeptical about a reform that has been heralded as enthusiastically as the Clean Money Option. But from a constitutional perspective, there is good reason for optimism. Of all the models of reform, the Clean Money

Clean and Constitutional

Option is the least susceptible to constitutional challenge—at least under current doctrine.

Buckley is most commonly understood as the case that equates money with speech. The Court's ruling in *Buckley* declared, in essence, that each dollar spent in support of speech is as protected as the spoken word that it buys. This principle, simple enough to state, has evolved into a treacherous tangle of rules that ensnare the unwary—and sometimes even the wary.

The *Buckley* decision's central prop is a distinction between expenditures and contributions. Expenditures, the Court held, are fully protected. That means that a Perot or a Huffington has an absolute right to buy his way into office. It means a fat cat has an absolute right to saturate the airwaves with a message advocating for or against a candidate. And a campaign has a right to spend unlimited amounts of money that it collects from others—so long as each contribution is in a permissible amount and from a legal source. Thus, in 1976 *Buckley* struck down mandatory caps on expenditures in congressional campaigns, and, in *Buckley*'s name, a federal court recently struck down a campaign expenditure cap imposed by the city of Cincinnati.

On the other hand, *contribution* caps are permitted—but only up to a point. No contribution cap has ever been sustained except on the rationale that it advances the battle against corruption or the appearance of corruption.

Following this rationale, only a contribution that is or would appear to be corrupting can be barred. Several courts have therefore struck down $100 contribution caps, on the theory that no politician is corrupted by a $101 contribution. Also under attack are caps on aggregate contributions from a type of source (out-of-state donors or PACs, for example), on the theory that all is well as long as no single contribution is independently corrupting.

So what does all this mean for the Clean Money Option? The crucial aspect of the Clean Money Option, from the perspective of constitutional doctrine, is that it essentially bribes candidates to do what they cannot be forced to do: to forego all contributions upon qualifying (the ultimate contribution limit) and to cap expenditures. Under *Buckley*, this "carrot" approach is permissible, so long as the candidate remains truly free to turn down the invitation. Applying this test, the *Buckley* Court upheld the presidential public financing system, under which presidential candidates receive a large pot of money (currently over $60 million each for major-party candidates) in return for foregoing all private funds and capping expenditures.

One would think, then, that almost any incentive would be upheld, right? Not so fast. Though the issue has scarcely been explored (because public financing systems are fairly uncommon), the courts have already begun to muddle the rules on at least two crucial points.

Clean and Constitutional

First, how enticing can the deal be? On the "if it works it must be unconstitutional" side of the ledger, is a case in which a federal court struck down an aspect of Kentucky's matching contribution plan. In the Kentucky plan, a candidate who accepted expenditure caps could raise campaign money in $500 chunks (which are matched with public funds), but a candidate who opted out was relegated to raising money in bite-sized $100 increments. A federal court, concluding that no candidate could afford to opt out under these terms, found this provision coercive. On the other side of the ledger are two recent federal appeals court decisions upholding Rhode Island's and Minnesota's partial financing schemes. The Rhode Island scheme contains a similar "cap gap" provision, with a two-to-one gap. And both the Rhode Island and the Minnesota schemes lift the expenditure caps entirely for a participating candidate once a nonparticipating opponent reaches a certain fund-raising or spending level. Neither was struck as coercive, although both are quite enticing.

An aspect of the Minnesota scheme that was struck down, however, raises the second set of issues, which could be critical to the success of the Clean Money Option. If past experience is any indication, the attempt to reduce the flow of money directly into political campaigns will simply lead influence-seekers to reroute their money by spending independently in support of candidates or by laundering large contributions through the party ("soft money"). The soft-money loophole can easily be closed, but the difficult constitutional question is how far can a public financing scheme go to discourage independent expenditures? The Maine system offers candidates more money if they come under considerable attack from independent expenditures. One federal court has already struck Minnesota's variant of this approach—a provision that freed any participating candidate to raise more money (with a government match of contributions) in response to a deluge of independent spending targeted against him or her. The better view is that under the First Amendment, helping a target of such "counter speech" is not punishment; rather, it is in the great First Amendment tradition that the best antidote to speech is more speech.

We must not allow the courts to make as much of a muddle out of the subsidy side of campaign finance regulation as they have of the restriction side. For now, from a constitutional perspective, the subsidy side of the field is the most promising of all, if only because the landmines have yet to be laid.

Labor's Role

STEVE ROSENTHAL AND AMANDA FUCHS

Real campaign finance reform must even the playing field so that any qualified candidate can run a viable campaign regardless of wealth or access to it.

The underlying problem of the current political system is that money has flooded the election process and has driven campaign spending out of control. The cost of campaigns has prevented ordinary people from having a fair shot at winning elective office. Today only the wealthy or well-connected can run viable races because only they are able to raise the enormous sums of money required to do so.

A look at the 1996 U.S. House of Representatives races exemplifies the role that wealthy contributors now play in political campaigns. The cost of winning the average U.S. House race has more than doubled in the last ten years. According to a study by Citizen Action, corporate special-interest PACs and large individual donors poured $459 million into House and Senate campaigns during the 1996 election cycle—giving Republican candidates $285 million (62 percent of these donations) and Democratic candidates $174 million (38 percent).

For many years, American working families have had virtually no voice in our political system. That is why, in 1996, organized labor undertook an unprecedented grassroots campaign to educate and mobilize working families around priority legislative issues. Called Labor '96, this campaign was part of a long-term effort to put the issues facing working families in the forefront of the national debate, to inform working Americans about incumbents' voting records on issues, and to hold elected leaders accountable for their actions.

Our campaign succeeded in putting working families' issues back on the table. After the Gingrich-led 104th Congress launched the worst assault on working families in seventy-five years—attacking virtually every right and protection that American workers possess—Labor '96's efforts forced many members of Congress to abandon the Gingrich "revolution." By exposing congressional votes against working families and by educating and mobilizing union members around key issues, the labor movement shifted the national debate, and issues such as retirement security, education, and Medicare became the defining issues of 1996.

As effective as labor's efforts were, working families were countered by a heavily funded attack by big business. During the 1996 election cycle, working families were outspent more than eleven to one by business groups. According to the Center for Responsive Politics (CRP), large corporate interests dominate the political process through PAC, individual, and soft-money contributions. Considering PAC spending alone, business PACs outspent labor three to one. An October 1996 CRP report stated, "No business-labor ratio tilts in favor of business even if the AFL-CIO's much reported $35 million in spending on issues ads is added to direct contributions."

The AFL-CIO endorses the idea of meaningful campaign finance reform that will ensure that ordinary Americans have a voice in the political process. Campaigns must be about people—not about money. In order for this to happen, the role of small contributors must be strengthened by reducing the role of wealthy contributors, including wealthy individuals and large corporate interests.

To do this, any meaningful campaign finance reform proposal must include public financing of campaigns. Public financing would reduce candidates' dependence on wealthy contributors and also eliminate candidates' need to spend all their time raising money.

As we work to reform campaign finance laws at the state and federal level, a possible model deserving consideration is the statewide initiative which was passed in Maine in November 1996. By combining full public financing, limits on what candidates can spend on campaigns, reduced contributions, and a shorter campaign season, the Maine law takes the political advantage away from the wealthy and gives ordinary voters a larger political voice.

We must also consider other models of election reform. It is clear that the American public is fed up with the role of money in politics. As we work towards shifting the focus of campaigns from money to people, we must take steps to increase voter participation. These efforts should include—but not be limited to—early voting, same-day registration, vote-by-mail, twenty-four-hour voting, and making election day a national holiday.

Donnelly, Fine, and Miller write that their proposal will mean "a fairer political system, with greater equality in opportunities for political influence." Working families deserve to have their voices heard—from the nation's state houses to the White House. Real reform must put the voters back in the driver's seat.

The Patriot Option

BRUCE ACKERMAN

Campaign reform lives in a time warp, untouched by the regulatory revolution of the last generation. The new regulators disdain heavy-handed "command and control" by bureaucrats. Rather than abolish markets, they try to reshape incentives to encourage socially responsible decision making. Unfortunately, neither the reformers in Congress nor the activists in Maine have tried to incorporate this new thinking into their campaign finance reform proposals.

The reform package now in Congress (the McCain-Feingold bill) is a tired repetition of familiar themes. It seeks to limit total campaign expenditures by targeting particular groups for specially restrictive treatment and rewarding cooperating candidates with free television time and reduced postage rates. This now traditional combination of expenditure limitation, subsidies, and regulatory scapegoating generates a series of familiar dangers. Maine's Clean Money Option also suffers from well-known troubles.

The Perils of Traditional Reform

By restricting the amount of money sloshing through the system, we create two big problems. Most obviously, we reduce the amount of political debate. While money isn't speech, it makes effective speech possible, especially in an age of mass media. Less money, less speech—this immediately generates anxious doubts. Do we really want equality at the cost of shutting down debate?

Restricting the flow of cash may also perversely affect the balance of power between incumbents and challengers. Incumbents go into campaigns with public reputations generated through years of high-visibility service. Challengers need lots of cash to offset this advantage. By placing an overall limit on funds, aren't we allowing old-timers to tighten their grip on office under the banner of "reform"?

McCain-Feingold also targets particular groups for particularly intensive regulation. PAC money is restricted in new ways that enhance bureaucratic intervention into areas that involve the nuts and bolts of the political process. The result will be a system that increases bureaucratic control and decreases the overall resources available for dynamic public debate.

Clean Money advocates are on solid ground, then, in criticizing the kind of partial reform represented by McCain-Feingold. But they too have failed to transcend "command and control" models. By giving each qualify-

The Patriot Option

ing candidate an equal amount of public money, they will force reformers to make an unacceptable choice. Either we will starve serious candidates like Bob Dole to limit the funding of fringe candidates like Alan Keyes, or we can fully fund Dole and provide the Keyeses of this world with massive doses of ego-gratification. Neither of these alternatives will prove palatable to the larger public.

Worse yet, the Clean Money advocates have built a large dose of incumbent protection into their program by insisting on short campaigns and reducing the overall level of funds. It would be tragic if a generation of activists wasted their energies on such a poorly elaborated scheme.

Reforming Reform

We have only primitive regulatory thinking to blame for this impasse. We can achieve genuine campaign reform at an acceptable price by relying on more innovative regulatory methods. The most promising system adapts the voucher technique that is already familiar from discussions of education and welfare reform.

When Americans register to vote, they should be issued a credit card by a special public company—call it the Patriot Card and color it red, white, and blue. This card will become the basis of campaign finance.

Suppose, for example, that each voter's card were automatically credited with a $25 balance for the presidential election in the year 2000. To gain access to this "red-white-and-blue" money, candidates and other political organizations would be obliged to demonstrate significant popular support by gathering an appropriate number of voter signatures. Upon receipt of these signatures, the Patriot Company would open an account that grants the candidate an initial balance of red-white-and-blue money—$1 million, say, for presidential aspirants. Candidates could then spend their initial stake on advertisements aiming to convince Patriot holders to transfer more red-white-and-blue money to them. Some candidates will, of course, soon see their initial Patriot balance shrink to zero; others will generate tens of millions as the campaign proceeds.

Under the Patriot program, only red-white-and-blue money could be legally used to finance political campaigns. The use of greenbacks would be treated as a form of corruption similar to the use of greenbacks to buy votes.

The resulting system would reduce the influence of private wealth without transferring power from the general citizenry to an imperial bureaucracy. It would also obviate the need to target PACs or other regulatory scapegoats. If the American Medical Association can convince doctors (or their patients) to transfer their ten red-white-and-blue dollars to Doctors for Good Government, rather than Citizens for Clinton or the Republican Party, so be it. Patriot does not prevent PACs from continuing to play the game of electoral politics, albeit on a reduced scale.

The Patriot Option

Finally, the reform should be designed to guarantee against any decline in overall resources flowing into the political marketplace. Congress should stipulate that each cardholder must receive an individual balance that, when summed together with everyone else's balance, greatly exceeds the total amount spent in the last green-money election. For example, if $25 in red-white-and-blue money were distributed to each of America's 130 million registered voters, the $3.25 billion deposited in Patriot accounts would be three times the amount spent in the last presidential election. Even if lots of people never used their Patriot cards, more money would still be running through the system.

In exchange, the voucher plan transforms campaign finance from an inegalitarian embarrassment into a new occasion for civic responsibility. Each Patriotic decision will serve as a preliminary vote—encouraging cardholders to focus on the campaign as it develops and support the candidates of their choice at the time of their choice. At the same time, it makes it virtually impossible for federal officials to disrupt the flow of funds going into particular campaigns.

Patriot is no panacea. But this is not the place to elaborate all the legal and technical questions raised in its operation. It is more important to urge reformers to rethink their regulatory philosophy before spending years of work on an obsolete agenda.

A Plea for Realism

THOMAS E. MANN

For several reasons I am absolutely delighted that Ellen Miller and her colleagues have launched a national campaign to spread the recently approved Maine system of voluntary full public financing of elections to other states. Efforts to reform our campaign finance system at the federal level have been frustrated in Washington for years, while the states have begun to experiment in a number of interesting and promising ways. If Ellen Miller, David Donnelly, and Janice Fine are correct that citizens are much more open to public financing than they are thought to be by national policymakers, what better way to demonstrate that reality than by garnering the support of citizens state by state for Maine-style financing?

It is indisputably true that worrisome inequities are present in our political system as a result of the way our campaigns are financed. One doesn't have to endorse every element of their diagnosis and prescription to acknowledge that Miller, her coauthors, and her associates in Public Campaign are raising immensely important questions about the health of our democracy. A full discussion and debate about the appropriate role of public versus private funds in our elections is welcome, although I am much less certain about the outcome of that debate than advocates of the Clean Money Option appear to be.

My doubts are based on a number of considerations. While it is not surprising that reformers tend to exaggerate in their claims about the impact of money in politics in order to stoke public outrage, hyperbolic language has the unfortunate side effect of raising public expectations sky-high. For example, the authors approvingly cite *The Nation*'s rendition of how political contributions provide a handsome return on investment for corporate America in the form of "direct corporate welfare" from the Commerce Department. Call me a radical, but am I the only reader who thought, "Come on. AT&T, Boeing, and General Electric would almost certainly have won the same benefits from Commerce without their measly campaign contributions"? I have the same reaction to the endless stories based on simple correlations between PAC contributions and votes in Congress. Take away every PAC dollar and I bet few votes would change on the House and Senate floors.

I am not arguing that private campaign contributions are ineffectual or that serious problems of conflict of interest do not arise. We ought to be concerned that moneyed interests are much more likely to attract the attention and energy of members of Congress than ordinary constituents and that the policy agendas of parties and officeholders are shaped by their constant scramble for campaign funds. Officeholders are consumed with fund-raising and the money chase does have harmful affects on our democracy. But overheated rhetoric that claims that politicians are routinely bought and sold by special interests and that private campaign money is the root of all evil in our democracy misleads citizens into expecting that full public financing will lead to dramatic changes in governance and policy. I think not. Inequalities in social and economic resources, even in the absence of private campaign contributions, would continue to shape politics and policy making in America. It is as much a mistake for reformers to overpromise as it is for politicians to do so.

I worry also whether a system of full public financing would work outside a friends-and-neighbors kind of state like Maine. It is difficult and expensive for candidates, especially challengers, to reach a largely disinterested and disengaged public. Would that same public be able to stomach spending the large amounts of tax dollars needed to broadcast a reasonable amount of information about the competing candidates? And what happens when candidates limited to their allotment of public funds are assaulted by forces operating outside the regulated system, exploiting issue advocacy or independent spending loopholes? (The response to the latter that has been built into the Maine system, providing up to twice the original amount of public funds to candidates under such an assault, seems woefully inadequate.) And what role would political parties play in a system of full public financing to candidates? Would they be rendered obsolete, further fueling the lone-ranger perspective of many politicians?

I suspect that the idea of full public financing will not sit well in a country whose political culture is as individualistic and anti-statist as ours is. We will likely insist on some serious test of popular support for candidates, in the form of private fund-raising, before they reap public campaign funds. We will probably also want to retain private contributions as means of expressing the intensity of political commitment and of channeling social action, which are hallmarks of our democracy. Still, having a lively test of these propositions should be welcomed. Let Ellen Miller and her colleagues press their case in states across the country.

As for me, I prefer to work on the here and now, on changes in law that would address some of the most egregious flaws in our system, which in 1996 precipitated a virtual collapse of the regulatory regime for campaign finance. This means banning soft money, limiting the blatant political abuse of "issue advocacy," providing broadcast time to candidates, encouraging small contributions, and strengthening disclosure and enforcement. These are achievable objectives if we spend some of our resources on reaching them.

A Role for Parties

DANIEL H. LOWENSTEIN

A collision between public and private interests has produced "a system gone awry," according to David Donnelly, Janice Fine, and Ellen Miller. Apparently, the authors are not fans of James Madison. In *The Federalist No. 10*, Madison argued persuasively that the clash of public and private interests is inevitable in a republic. No measures short of the destruction of liberty could prevent it.

It is to be expected that private interests will deploy whatever resources are at hand to influence public policy. *Of course* corporations, unions, and other interests will use campaign contributions—and other measures far more potent than campaign contributions—to further their interests. And *of course* articulate individuals such as Donnelly, Fine, and Miller will resort to hyperbole when seeking support for *their* proposed policies. Those who believe that politics should resemble a learned debating society may look askance at such activities; Madisonians will recognize them as symptoms not of democratic failure but of democracy itself.

A Role for Parties

Despite its exaggerations and its shaky foundation, Donnelly, Fine, and Miller's essay contains much that is of value. Although the consequences for public policy are not nearly as great as they suggest, they correctly assert that the present system of campaign finance gives rise to widespread conflicts of interest.[1] Most importantly, they concisely demonstrate some of the major flaws in the proposed reforms that have dominated recent debates on campaign finance.

Donnelly, Fine, and Miller support what they call the Clean Money Option, a version of which has been enacted by Maine voters. Under this system, candidates will be encouraged to agree to spending limits in return for their campaign funds being almost entirely provided by the state.

If you glance at a map you will quickly notice that Maine is very far away from California, where I reside. I cannot say how the Clean Money Option will work in Maine, but I sincerely hope it will have beneficial effects.

There are many differences, however, between Maine and California besides geographical location. Among the most important are that they have more lobsters and we have more people. Whatever the effects of the Clean Money Option may be in Maine, I am afraid it would be quite harmful in the unlikely event it were applied on a larger scale, such as in congressional elections or in big states like California.[2]

I have this fear primarily because of what I believe are the answers to three questions that Donnelly, Fine, and Miller never even consider:

1. How much will the Clean Money Option cost?
2. Will the amounts made available to candidates be sufficient for vigorous, competitive campaigns?
3. Who will decide, and on what basis, how much will be spent in campaigns?

These questions are interrelated. The answer to the third, presumably, is that the amount to be spent in campaigns will be decided either by the state legislature or by the electorate in initiative campaigns such as the one in Maine. Either way, there will be a strong bias toward low amounts, for several reasons: the political and budgetary need to keep public costs down (see Question 1); the widespread perception, exploited by writers like Donnelly, Fine, and Miller, that "too much" is spent on campaigns; and the benefit to incumbents of keeping campaign expenditures below a competitive level. Since no reason appears as to why the setting of campaign spending limits should be exempt from the forces of self-interest and demagoguery that attend most political decision making, it is predictable that the answer to Question 2 would then be a distinct *no*.

I asked a couple of California campaign consultants (one Democrat and one Republican) what they would regard as an appropriate amount to spend for a talented but not well-known candidate challenging an incumbent in a competitive, high-turnout California congressional district. The lower of the two figures I received was $800,000. If that amount were given to each of two candidates in each House district nationwide, the cost would be nearly $700 million. Add about two-thirds as much for the Senate elections that take place in a given election year, and the total—with nothing included for primaries or independent or third-party candidates—would be well over $1 billion for a two-year cycle. Congress is very unlikely to spend so much.

In addition, the Clean Money Option would be disastrous for electoral competition, which according to Donnelly, Fine, and Miller should be enhanced by campaign finance regulation. One of the most consistent findings in political science research over the last two decades is that challengers typically need to spend large amounts to have a chance to defeat incumbents. The Clean Money Option encourages incumbent legislators to guarantee their own electoral security by limiting their challengers' campaigns.

Even if incumbents' self-interest did not prevent the funding of campaigns at fully competitive levels, ordinary principles of fiscal prudence would do so. To pay two candidates in *every* district the amount that challengers could usefully spend in the most competitive districts would be extremely wasteful. For this reason, many public financing proposals work by matching private contributions with public funds. But for a number of reasons, some of which are well stated by Donnelly, Fine, and Miller, matching is also an inefficient means of allocating public funding.

What is needed is an allocation of public funds based on reliable political judgment of where the money can be used to enhance electoral competition. Obviously, no government agency can be trusted to make such judgments, so reformers have assumed that they must employ mechanical allocation devices, all of which are seriously flawed.

But sensible allocation of funds *is* possible, by the simple expedient of entrusting that allocation to the political parties. Such a system would provide vastly more bang for the public buck than any of the typical public funding schemes proposed by reformers, including the Clean Money Option. Because of its more efficient allocation of funds, such a system would increase the level of electoral competition while minimizing the reliance on private contributions that causes conflicts of interest.

Space does not permit setting forth the details of such a plan, but I have done so in my article "On Campaign Finance Reform: The Root of All Evil Is Deeply Rooted,"[3] and I will be glad to send copies on request. One point should be added here. Neither the Clean Money Option nor any of the reform ideas that Donnelly, Fine, and Miller criticize addresses the fundamen-

A Role for Parties

tal cause of the campaign finance problem. That fundamental cause is the need for voters to receive information on large numbers of candidates. Voters increasingly believe they should vote for the "best candidate" rather than for the party. Whatever else may be said about this idea, it vastly increases the information needs of the voter. But most voters are turned off to politics and do not seek out such information. Candidates have no choice but to spend ever greater sums to force information into unreceptive minds.

The campaign finance problem is in large part the result of a candidate-oriented rather than a party-oriented electoral system. Public financing channeled through party leaders, in addition to its great advantages in terms of efficiency, would be a small step in the direction of a cheaper, more accountable electoral system, which is to say a more party-oriented system.

III

Reply

DAVID DONNELLY, JANICE FINE,
AND ELLEN S. MILLER

The respondents to our essay share our goal: a political system "of, by, and for the people." We all agree, too, that fundamental changes will be needed to achieve this goal, that working together is important, and that (to paraphrase Senator Russell Feingold) reform will take patience and steadfastness in the face of tremendous opposition.

It is clear, however, that we have substantial differences on how best to reform the political system. We have absolutely no intention of claiming that the Clean Money Option alone will bring us there. Indeed it is, as our respondents suggest, only one of a series of steps to restore vitality to our democratic process. But two of the routes to reform suggested in the replies are, as we see it, not worth taking. One would require that the Supreme Court change its mind about *Buckley*, or that the Constitution be amended. The second is partial reform, which would lead us somewhere, but not necessarily to where we want to go. We will consider these in turn, and then discuss some of the criticisms that have been voiced about the Clean Money Option itself.

First, because there's little hope of overturning the Supreme Court's decision in *Buckley* in the short term, effective reform requires that we work within its confines. This rules out many otherwise worthy proposals. In particular, as Josh Rosencranz argues, the courts are looking less favorably upon restrictions (campaign contribution limits) than upon subsidies (providing voluntary public financing). Low contribution limits, as urged by Doug Phelps and passed by Arkansas voters, have been thrown out by courts in Missouri, the District of Columbia, and Oregon. Similarly, Bruce Ackerman's Patriot program—if it includes the provision that "only red-white-and-blue money could be legally used to finance political campaigns"—would also need constitutional modification or reinterpretation. Some provisions of McCain-Feingold—in-district funding requirements and bans on PACs—are also constitutionally suspect. We must do more than write our victories in the sand. (Here we must simply disagree with Phelps's assertion that the Clean Money Option itself will require a constitutional amendment or the overturning of *Buckley*. A recent 8th Circuit decision, in *Rosensteil v. Rodriguez*, is promising on this score.)

As to a constitutional amendment limiting campaign spending: while we agree in principle, we just don't think

Reply

it is a practical strategy. What we hope, however, is that if organizations like USPIRG (the United States Public Interest Research Group) pursue it, they will not exclude other strategies. Even with a constitutional change, we would still need to enact meaningful reform addressing the source of campaign money. It is this process—the state-by-state efforts and the passage of federal reform—that will set the stage for the day that the *Buckley* decision is relegated to history.

Second, just because the road to reform has some constitutional obstacles in it doesn't mean that reformers should settle for partial measures. As John Stuart Mill said, "Against a great evil a small remedy does not produce a small result, it produces no result at all." The proposals outlined by several of the respondents deal inadequately with the most direct and corrosive aspect of our political system—the special-interest financing of our elected officials. That is what the Clean Money Option addresses, and it does so simply. Additional provisions, like Senator Feingold's soft-money and independent expenditure proposals are essential, and would be included in any federal Clean Money bill.

Third, apart from proposing alternative reform strategies, the respondents raise certain questions about the Clean Money proposal itself. Zach Polett observes that we don't want systems that increase the power of politicians while diminishing that of organized groups of voters. We couldn't agree more. By requiring that candidates collect a large number of small contributions to qualify for public funding, the Clean Money Option would create a system in which grassroots organizations of all types, as well as political parties, could be at the center. Money shouldn't be the only vehicle for accountability, though. Steve Rosenthal and Amanda Fuchs understand this as well, and we appreciate their willingness to support proposals along the lines of Maine's initiative.

Thomas Mann raises similar questions, and also underscores the need to address independent expenditures. We agree that there is such a need. While the Maine law doubles the public money given to complying candidates in response to this type of spending, the federal proposal caps that amount at a fivefold increase. What are the implications of this for the problem of costs raised by Daniel Lowenstein? Clean Money federal elections will cost the average taxpayer less per year than the price of a movie ticket and bag of popcorn. And certainly today's underfunded challengers will fare better in a Clean Money framework.

Lowenstein also asks about party-strengthening measures. We are all for them. The soft-money drug isn't strengthening our major parties. It has turned them into corporate money junkies, looking for the next hundred-thousand-dollar fix. That's why we wholeheartedly agree with Senator Feingold's soft-money provision, and would support it—in a heartbeat—as a stand-alone provision.

As for James Madison: According to Lowenstein's reading, American democracy is *supposed* to be a collision of private and public interests. We prefer to listen to Madison when he directly addresses the central role of money in politics: "Who are to be the electors of the federal representatives? Not the rich more than the poor; not the learned more than the ignorant; not the haughty heirs of distinguished names more than the humble sons [and daughters] of obscure and unpropitious fortune."

Notes

David Donnelly, Janice Fine, and Ellen S. Miller / *Going Public*

1. Our discussion of these flows draws principally on research and documentation by the Center for Responsive Politics. See their website at http://www.crp.org, especially *The Big Picture: Who Paid for the Last Election*.

2. Doug Ireland, "Daley's Commerce: William Daley Seems to Fit Ron Brown's Shoes—A Master of 'Pinstripe Patronage,'" *The Nation*, 3 February 1997.

3. Thomas A. Barnard, "One Step Forward, Two Steps Back: The Progress of Campaign Finance Reform in Washington" (Institute for Washington's Future, 1996).

4. The Working Group was a small think tank of organizers and researchers that came together to develop realistic proposals for campaign finance reform.

Douglas Phelps / *Setting Limits*

1. McCain-Feingold invites candidates to accept its system of voluntary spending limits by, among other things, *doubling* current contribution limits from $1,000 to $2,000. Other laudable attributes of the legislation are undone by this institutionalization of fat-cat influence.

2. Numerous recent studies document the very high correlation between success in fund-raising and success on election day, and also reveal that most campaign money comes in the form of large checks from a tiny, wealthy percentage of the population.

3. Corporate contributions to candidates have been banned in

federal elections since 1907, but so-called soft-money loopholes have been opened up in the last twenty years to render the prohibition meaningless. Worse yet, in many states, corporations *can* give directly to candidates. In California, corporations alone give more than eight times the total amount from all donors contributing less than $100. (California Public Interest Research Group, *Elections, Inc.: How Democracy Has Become Corporatocracy in California*, 10 September 1996, p. 3.)

4. In 1994 in California, for example, candidates for state office who raised the most money won 96 percent of the time. (California Public Interest Research Group, *Sacramento for Sale: A CALPIRG Study of Contributions to California Legislative and Statewide Candidates in the 1994 Election Cycle*, 19 September 1996, p. 4.)

5. In 1994 in California, for example, candidates for legislative and statewide offices raised a whopping 97 percent of campaign funds from contributors giving $100 or more; 84 percent came from contributors of $1,000 or more. (Ibid.)

6. Observes Kevin Phillips, "Policy in Washington is now made by what we can justly call the 'venal center.' This is where the people who gave the national Republican Party a record $549 million during the 1995–96 election cycle overlap with the contributors, many of them the same wealthy Americans, who gave the national Democratic Party $332 million in the same period. . . . The influence of money is driving out the influence of voters." (Kevin Phillips, "The Venal Center," *Los Angeles Times*, 23 February 1997, p. M1.)

7. I view the Maine initiative as more indicative of its sponsors' laudable coalition-building skills than the underlying popularity of the idea. Donnelly, Fine, and Miller cite public opinion polls to suggest that voters support public financing. Yet in their narrative on the Maine experience, they seem to acknowledge considerable voter antipathy for the idea, and emphasize the tactical importance of characterizing it "merely as a means" to get special interest money out of politics, with greater public emphasis placed on this latter goal. Perhaps another interpretation of available polling might be that voters seem increasingly willing to *accept* public financing if it is linked to getting big money out of politics and if little mention is made of any

cost to taxpayers. Some experts regard even that statement as generous.

8. Winning low-limits initiatives received 77 percent of the vote in Missouri (1994), 72 percent in Oregon (1994), 66 percent in Colorado (1996) and in Arkansas (1996), 65 percent in Washington, D.C. (1992), 63 percent in Montana (1994), and 61 percent in California (in 1994, even with support dividing between two competing low-limits alternatives on the ballot).

9. The California initiative was sold to voters as a "low-limits" strategy to limit the influence of big money in politics. It is worth noting, however, that it was actually drafted primarily to try to hold down spending by inducing candidates to accept voluntary spending limits with offers of big money incentives. By allowing fat cats and even corporations to double their contributions to candidates who accept spending limits, and also allowing huge contributions to political parties (which can then pass this money on to candidates), while severely limiting small-donor PACs, Proposition 208 will actually worsen the ratio of big money to small contributions. (See California Public Interest Research Group, *Proposition 208: A Sheep in Wolf's Clothing; A CALPIRG Analysis of Prop. 208's Flaws, Loopholes, Drafting Errors, and Omissions*, 17 October 1996.)

10. For an excellent recent discussion of campaign limits and the Constitution, see Ronald Dworkin, "The Curse of American Politics," *New York Review of Books*, 17 October 1996, pp. 19–24.

11. Such an amendment has been repeatedly introduced in Congress for years by Senator Hollings of South Carolina, though it unnecessarily hamstrings itself by placing the word "reasonable" before "limits." Congress is considered unlikely to pass such an amendment until there is serious momentum towards a Constitutional Convention, the alternative route to amending the Constitution which has historically been necessary to prompt congressional action on amendments.

12. Judicial obtuseness on this point should be considered in light of the fact that judges are, after all, creatures of the system, appointed by politicians who are winners under the current campaign financing rules.

Notes

DANIEL H. LOWENSTEIN / *A Role for Parties*

1. As I have previously argued, it is usually more accurate to think of campaign finance in terms of conflicts of interest than in terms of corruption or, worse, the appearance of corruption. See my article "On Campaign Finance Reform: The Root of All Evil Is Deeply Rooted," *Hofstra Law Review* 18 [1989]: 301–67. The same article contains a detailed proposal for campaign finance regulation along the lines suggested briefly at the end of the present commentary.

2. Ironically, the system is well suited to the largest-scale election of all, the presidential election. The reason is that presidential elections do not depend on campaign spending by challengers in order to be competitive.

3. See note 1 to this essay, above, for complete citation.

ABOUT THE CONTRIBUTORS

BRUCE ACKERMAN is Sterling Professor of Law and Political Science at Yale University. His most recent books are *We the People*, vol. 2 (Harvard University Press, 1998), and *The Case Against Lameduck Impeachment* (Seven Stories, 1999).

DAVID DONNELLY is the former campaign manager for Maine Voters for Clean Elections. He works with the Northeast Citizen Action Resource Center on state-based reform.

RUSSELL FEINGOLD, a Democrat, is the junior United States Senator from Wisconsin. He is the coauthor, with Senator John McCain (Republican, Arizona), of the bipartisan McCain-Feingold campaign reform finance bill.

JANICE FINE is the organizing director for the Northeast Citizen Action Resource Center and a Ph.D. candidate in political science at the Massachusetts Institute of Technology.

AMANDA FUCHS is a researcher in the AFL-CIO's Political Department. She served as the Midwest press secretary for Labor '96.

DANIEL H. LOWENSTEIN is a professor at the UCLA Law School. His *Election Law* is the first American textbook on its subject to be published in the twentieth century.

THOMAS E. MANN is the director of the Governmental Studies Program at the Brookings Institution.

ELLEN S. MILLER is the former executive director of the Center for Responsive Politics and the director of the new reform group Public Campaign.

DOUGLAS PHELPS is the chairman of the United States Public Interest Research Group (USPIRG).

About the Contributors

ZACH POLETT, an Arkansas resident, serves as the director of political operations for the Association of Community Organizations for Reform Now (ACORN).

E. JOSHUA ROSENKRANZ is the executive director of the Brennan Center for Justice at New York University School of Law. The center's Democracy Program provides legal counseling and litigation support on campaign finance issues.

STEVE ROSENTHAL is the Political Director of the AFL-CIO. He has worked as a labor and political organizer for years and has served as campaign manager and consultant in numerous congressional, state, and local races.

JK
1991
.D67

1999